Forgive Them, Ethan!

Forgive Them, Ethan!

The Tragic Story of an Ordinary Family Who Didn't Know How to Talk About Love

Liudmila Pirojenko

Forgive Them, Ethan!
© Liudmila Pirojenko, 2024.
All rights reserved

Table of Contents

Introduction

THE WINTER wind howled outside, a relentless lament resonating with Ethan's chest ache. Beyond the frosted window, the world was stripped of color, a somber tableau of white snow and ash-gray skies. The streets lay under a thick, unbroken blanket of snow, muffling even the faintest hum of life and leaving an almost unnatural quiet behind. The silence pressed into the room, amplifying the heaviness in Ethan's heart.

By the window, Ethan sat motionless, his eyes locked on the barren trees standing like sentinels in the distance. Their frost-coated branches stretched toward the heavens, skeletal and brittle, as though pleading for something they knew would never come. The bitter cold radiated through the glass, sneaking into the room and winding its way through his body, chilling him from the outside in. It wasn't far from how his grief worked—an all-encompassing frost that refused to thaw, numbing him to everything but the void that had taken root deep within.

The scene outside echoed his inner world, an unrelenting winter of the soul. His thoughts felt frozen, stuck in an endless loop of pain, regret, and questions that would never be answered. The laughter and love of the past felt as unreachable as the warmth of summer in this barren season.

Ethan exhaled slowly, his breath fogging the window in a brief, fragile warmth before vanishing just as quickly.

Liudmila Pirojenko

The weight of his emotions was constant, like the snowdrifts that piled against the streets—unmoving, relentless, and suffocating. He closed his eyes briefly and leaned against the frosty pane as if searching for a crack, a way out, a thaw in the endless winter within and around him. But all he found was the unyielding cold and the endless howling wind.

The Unraveling

IN THE prosperous enclave of Maplewood, where meticulously trimmed hedges bordered imposing estates, a young woman named Clara resided under the guardianship of her opulent aunt, Margaret. Clara, a spirited and aspiring eighteen-year-old, diligently pursued her studies to become a nurse. Yet, in the shadow of her aunt's towering social influence lay an unspoken edict that suffused her existence: she was expected to wed before the ink of her eighteenth year dried.

This societal decree loomed ever larger when a proposal arrived from Richard, a steadfast local officer ten years her senior. Though his nature was affable and his dedication to his duty unyielding, Clara bristled inwardly at the prospect of relinquishing her dreams for the suffocating mold of matrimony. Nevertheless, tethered by a sense of familial obligation, she acquiesced. Their nuptials unfolded in resplendent grandeur, and not long after, Clara bore their first child, a son named Ethan.

Ethan, a spirited reflection of his father, possessed Richard's outward demeanor and restless energy. His cleverness, tinged with impishness, often led to trouble at school. For Clara, however, her son's playful defiance mirrored a more profound dissatisfaction—an embodiment of what she perceived as Richard's lack of aspiration. Over time, another child joined their family, a daughter named Lily, who emerged as the quintessence of Clara's qualities—radiant, self-assured, and fiercely autonomous. Clara's latent discontent crystallized into resentment toward Ethan, and she increasingly directed her frustrations at him.

Meanwhile, steadfast and unassuming, Richard remained a devoted husband and father, his calm demeanor masking the turmoil within their home. He cherished his family and found contentment in their simple life, unaware of Clara's unrest. As Clara and Lily's bond deepened, their disdain for Richard and Ethan solidified into a toxic alliance. Their sharp tongues cut deeply, ridiculing the house's men and belittling their worth. Stung and bewildered, Ethan sought refuge in his father's unwavering support. Yet, in his loyalty, even Richard defended Clara, insisting that her love for their son was genuine despite her harshness.

Clara, a woman bound by the chains of societal expectations and the haunting echoes of her past, struggled profoundly with the concept of love. Though capable of great affection, her heart had been hardened by years of silent suffering, a fortress built to protect a wounded soul. Her childhood had been a mosaic of deprivation and dismissal, each fragment a painful reminder of her place in the world.

Born into a large, impoverished family, Clara's early years were defined by scarcity—not just material needs but affection and affirmation. Her parents, overwhelmed by the sheer weight of raising numerous children, viewed her less as an individual and more as another mouth to feed. When their burden grew too heavy, Clara was sent away to live with her stern, affluent aunt. The move was framed as an opportunity for a better life, but it felt like abandonment to Clara. It was a wound she carried silently, a whisper of unworthiness that echoed through her life.

In her aunt's house, perfection was not a virtue but a demand. Mistakes were met with cold reprimands, and achievements were acknowledged only insofar as they upheld appearances. This relentless pursuit of flawlessness became Clara's measure of self-worth, an unyielding yardstick against which she would later measure her children.

As a mother, Clara's parenting reflected her upbringing—rigid, demanding, and exacting. She sought to create a family that could not be criticized, children who would embody the perfection she had been forced to pursue. But the scars of her past had twisted her perception of love, confusing control with care and discipline with devotion.

Ethan, her son, bore the brunt of this distorted love. His free-spirited nature clashed with her rigid ideals, his individuality an affront to the conformity she sought to instill. Clara interpreted his defiance as a failure, a reflection of her inadequacies as a mother. In her frustration, she resorted to punitive measures, her anger masking the deep fear of losing control. She believed that molding him into her vision of success was an act of love, even as the emotional and physical toll on both of them grew heavier.

On the other hand, her daughter understood their household's unspoken rules. Shrewd and calculating, she learned to easily navigate her mother's insecurities. She became what Clara needed her to be—a reflection of perfection, a child who could uphold the family's fragile facade. But beneath her polished exterior lay a sharp cunning, a manipulative streak that fed on Clara's vulnerabilities. While Ethan sought authentic love and acceptance, his sister thrived in the toxic dynamic, weaponizing Clara's fears and expectations for her benefit.

Clara's inability to bridge the emotional chasm with her son wasn't born out of malice but ignorance and pain. She didn't know how to love without conditions because she had never been loved that way. Her heart carried a reservoir of unspoken tenderness, but it was buried beneath years of conditioning, fear, and a desperate need to protect herself from the vulnerability of unconditional love.

In her attempts to perfect her children, Clara unwittingly perpetuated the same cycles of neglect and misunderstanding that had shaped her own life. And yet, within her flaws and failings remained a glimmer of humanity—a woman who, despite everything, still yearned to love and be loved, even if she couldn't find the words or ways to express it.

The years turned, and the fissures in their family widened. The household became a battleground, with Clara and Lily reigning as an unyielding coalition of derision while Ethan struggled to navigate the hostile terrain. Desperate for escape, he was ensnared by loyalty and circumstance, unable to break free.

Then came an evening that would forever alter the trajectory of their lives. Ethan returned home to find pandemonium. Richard lay prostrate on the floor, his body convulsed in agony, while Clara and Lily stood to the side, their laughter cruel and discordant. The surreal tableau seared into Ethan's mind—a grotesque symphony of indifference to his father's plight. Despite the efforts of an emergency physician, Richard had endured both a stroke and a heart attack. Against the odds, he survived, but his body was left fragile and partially paralyzed.

Equipped with her medical training, Clara assumed the role of caregiver, though her ministrations were laced with acrimony. She nursed Richard's body while bruising his spirit, her bitterness seeping into every act of care. Her resentment deepened, casting a pall over the home. Ethan bore silent witness to his father's arduous recovery, a journey marked by physical struggle and emotional torment. Clara's venomous tirades, often bolstered by Lily's complicity, left Ethan torn between his father's vulnerability and the oppressive toxicity of the household.

Finally, the weight of his family's dysfunction proved insurmountable. Now a young man with a burning need to forge his path, Ethan departed for a distant city, yearning to escape the oppressive shadow of his mother and sister. Yet even in his newfound freedom, the scars of his upbringing followed him like an unshakable specter.

Clara's discontent reached its zenith when she chose to relocate, leaving her debilitated husband behind in their once-vibrant home. She claimed to be aiding distant relatives, but the truth lay bare—she abandoned Richard, isolating him in his infirmity. Their grand home, once a symbol of prosperity and promise, became a hushed tomb, holding the echoes of betrayal and fractured love within its walls.

The Aftermath

BUT GRIEF can bend time, stretching moments into eternity and collapsing days into fragments. As the nights grew longer, Ethan's apartment seemed to shrink around him, the silence swelling until it felt almost alive, pressing against his chest. The once-familiar space became oppressive, its quiet corners filled with echoes of words unsaid and regrets too heavy to voice. It was during these restless nights, when sleep became a reluctant visitor that the dreams began.

In the first dream, Richard appeared in a room bathed in an ethereal light, which seemed to come from everywhere and nowhere. He stood tall, his figure whole and unbroken, starkly contrasting to the weakened man Ethan had last seen. His father's face was calm and serene, but his eyes carried the weight of something more profound—quiet wisdom shaped by suffering. His voice was gentle when he spoke, like the soft murmur of leaves in the wind, yet it carried an undeniable force, a gravity that pulled at Ethan's very soul.

"Ethan," Richard said, his tone firm but tender, "you must let go of the anger. Holding onto it will only hurt you."

Ethan woke with a start, his heart racing and his skin clammy with sweat. The dream lingered, vivid and raw, as if his father's presence had been more than a figment of his imagination. He sat in the darkness, the room's stillness broken only by the clock ticking on the wall. Richard's words repeated in his mind, an insistent whisper that refused to fade. But how could he forgive?

How could he release the anger that had become a part of him, woven into his grief?

The dreams continued, each one more vivid than the last. Richard often stood in familiar places in them—a sunlit kitchen, the garden where he once toiled, or the living room where they had spent quiet evenings together. Yet these settings were imbued with an otherworldly quality, as though time had softened their edges, blurring reality into something almost sacred. His father's voice remained steady calm, yet unyielding in its message.

"Ethan," Richard urged, his eyes meeting his son's with an intensity that seemed to pierce through layers of grief and guilt. "The anger will consume you, just as it consumed them. You have to forgive. Not for them, but for yourself."

Ethan often woke from these dreams trembling, his breath coming in short, shallow gasps. The visions left him disoriented, caught between the vivid world of his father's words and the cold, unyielding reality of his apartment. Richard's presence in the dreams was a balm, offering a fleeting sense of comfort and connection, but it also became a source of torment. The thought of forgiving Clara and Lily felt impossible, a betrayal of the man whose suffering they had exacerbated. Yet, Richard's words carried a weight that Ethan could not ignore, a quiet insistence that forgiveness was not for their sake but for his salvation.

As the dreams grew more frequent, they began to shift. In one particularly vivid vision, Ethan stood in the family home, the walls peeling and the air heavy with a sense of decay. Richard appeared, seated in his old armchair, his posture relaxed but his expression serious. "Look around you, Ethan," he said, gesturing to the crumbling surroundings. "This is what anger does it eats away at everything, leaving nothing but ruins. You cannot live here, in this place of resentment. You must leave it behind."

The words struck Ethan like a hammer, shattering the fragile defenses he had built around his pain. He awoke with tears streaming down his face, his chest heaving with the weight of unspoken emotions. He longed for the peace his father seemed to offer in those dreams, but the path to it felt insurmountable, blocked by the towering walls of his anger and grief.

Each dream brought him closer to a choice he wasn't ready to make. The anger that had once fueled his resolve now felt like a heavy chain, binding him to a past he could neither change nor escape. Yet, the thought of letting it go felt equally unbearable, as though forgiving Clara and Lily would somehow diminish the pain Richard had endured.

Ethan found himself at a crossroads, the dreams pressing him toward a decision he couldn't avoid. Forgiveness was no longer just a concept—it had become a haunting refrain, a specter that visited him each night, urging him to relinquish the burden he had carried for so long. But in the quiet moments before dawn, as he sat alone in the shadows, he wondered: could he ever truly let go? Or would the weight of his past remain an unshakable anchor, dragging him deeper into the darkness?

The Journey to Forgiveness

AFTER months of wrestling with his emotions and carrying the weight of unresolved pain, Ethan made the pivotal decision to seek help. He began therapy, stepping into the quiet space of reflection and guidance, hoping to untangle the complex web of resentment, sorrow, and guilt that had consumed him for so long. His therapist, a compassionate yet firm guide, helped him confront the raw truths he had buried.

"It's natural to feel anger, Ethan," his therapist told him during one session, her tone steady yet kind. "But when you hold onto that anger, it becomes a chain, binding you to the pain you're trying to escape. Forgiveness isn't about excusing what they've done—it's about setting yourself free."

Those words struck a chord deep within him. Slowly, through countless sessions, Ethan began to peel back the layers of his grief and anger, examining each one with a mix of discomfort and curiosity. He unearthed the roots of Clara's cruelty, recognizing for the first time that her behavior wasn't born of malice alone but of deep-seated insecurities and unaddressed unhappiness. As for Lily, Ethan started to view her not as a villain but as another victim—someone shaped by the same toxic environment that had left its scars on him.

Ethan's perspective shifted as he reflected on his father's enduring kindness and love. Richard had always defended Clara, even in the face of her sharp words and relentless bitterness. It puzzled Ethan until one quiet evening when a realization washed over him.

Liudmila Pirojenko

Ethan's fingers trembled slightly across the faded script on the brittle, yellowed page. Richard's handwriting's familiar loops and curves tugged at something deep within him, a bittersweet blend of comfort and loss. It had been years since he had seen those distinct strokes, yet they felt as vivid as his father's voice.

As he read, the words unfolded like a window into Richard's soul—a place Ethan had rarely been allowed to see in life. The journal was not just a collection of memories but a testament to his father's silent battles, his unspoken grief, and his relentless capacity to love. Page by page, Ethan discovered the layers of a man who had carried the weight of pain while still choosing tenderness.

One particular entry stopped Ethan cold as though the words had reached out to grip his heart. Richard had written about the cracks in his marriage, the fractures that had widened into chasms. He described moments of feeling invisible, unwanted, and despised but also admitted that he had clung to hope like a lifeline. His faith in love, despite the heartbreak, was unshakable.

"I've often felt like an outsider in my own home," the entry read, the ink smudged as though blurred by tears. "But love isn't always about being seen or appreciated. Sometimes, it's about staying when it's easier to leave, forgiving when it's easier to hate. Love can be the only thing that keeps us alive, even when it hurts."

Ethan felt his chest tighten as he read the words. His father's pain was raw, etched into the pages with a candor that Ethan had never known. But what struck him most was the resilience—Richard's refusal to let bitterness consume him, his choice to keep loving even when it seemed futile.

For the first time, Ethan saw his father not just as a quiet, gentle figure in the background but as a man who had fought his wars. A man who had struggled with anger, rejection, and heartbreak, yet had somehow found his way to forgiveness—not for others' sake, but for his peace.

As Ethan gently closed the journal, he sat in silence, letting the weight of Richard's words settle over him. At that moment, he felt a connection to his father that he had never known. It was as though Richard's voice echoed in the stillness, urging him toward a path of healing and understanding.

Ethan realized that his father's wisdom was a guide, a map through the wilderness of his own emotions. He knew he couldn't change the past or erase the hurt caused by those he loved. But he could choose how to carry it. He could choose love, even when it felt impossible.

A newfound resolve swelled within him. Ethan promised himself that he would practice the patience his father had once shown, even in the face of rejection. He would strive to love unconditionally—not just others but himself, too. Most of all, he would embrace forgiveness, not as a gift to those who had wronged him, but as a liberation from the chains of resentment.

With the journal cradled, Ethan rose and stepped toward the window. The frost outside seemed to glimmer with a faint light as if the world was shifting, thawing. For the first time in a long time, Ethan felt a tiny spark of warmth within him, a flicker of hope that he could find peace.

"He loved her," Ethan murmured to himself, his voice barely audible in the stillness of his apartment. "Even when she didn't deserve it. Maybe that's what I need to do—not love them blindly but from afar. Love them enough to forgive without letting them hurt me again."

With this newfound clarity, Ethan put his thoughts and emotions into words. He began writing letters to Clara and Lily—not as a means to confront them, but as a way to unburden his heart. He poured everything onto the pages: his pain, his anger, his confusion, but also his desire to move forward. He wrote about their shared past, the moments of joy that still lingered amidst the sorrow, and the wounds that had defined their family.

Most importantly, Ethan extended forgiveness—not because their actions were justified, but because he was tired of carrying the heavy burden of anger. He didn't expect reconciliation or even a response. Writing and sending the letters was enough to mark the beginning of his healing.

When he finally mailed the letters, Ethan felt a strange sense of release, as though a long-carried weight had been lifted from his shoulders. It wasn't a dramatic moment of clarity but a quiet one, like a small crack in the dam of his emotions, letting light and air seep through. Over the following weeks, Ethan focused inward. He rediscovered passions that had been overshadowed by his pain, filling his days with creative pursuits, moments of laughter with friends, and activities that nourished his mental health.

Eventually, a letter arrived from Clara. It was not the response Ethan had hoped for. Her words were defensive, riddled with anger and denial. She dismissed much of what he had written, blaming him for abandoning the family and accusing him of misunderstanding her struggles. Yet, hidden between the barbs and recriminations, Ethan saw something unexpected—a flicker of vulnerability. She wrote about her regrets, her pain, and the difficulties she had faced in her life.

For the first time, Ethan saw Clara not as the cold, domineering figure of his childhood but as a flawed, broken human being. Her anger was a shield, her cruelty a symptom of her inner turmoil. This realization didn't excuse her behavior but softened Ethan's heart. He now understood that forgiveness wasn't a single moment but an ongoing process—a series of choices to let go, accept, and heal.

Ethan also recognized that forgiveness didn't have to mean reconciliation. He didn't have to reopen the door to Clara and Lily if doing so would harm his peace. He learned forgiveness was about freeing himself from the shadows of their actions, allowing himself to step fully into the light of his own life.

Ethan carried this truth forward, using it as a foundation to continue building a life unbound by his past. Though the scars of his childhood would always remain, they no longer defined him. Instead, they became reminders of his strength, resilience, and capacity to choose a different path.

The Healing

MONTHS turned into years, and Ethan focused on rebuilding himself from within. He poured his energy into his career, excelling in his field and carving out a life defined by purpose and self-discovery. Along the way, he found love, a partner who brought light into the corners of his heart, still shadowed by the pain of his past. Yet, no matter how far he moved forward, the memories of Richard lingered—his father's quiet resilience, suffering, and the unspoken words that seemed to echo in Ethan's mind.

Determined to process the turmoil within, Ethan began writing in a journal, pouring out the thoughts and emotions that had remained unspoken for years. Page by page, he chronicled the wounds of his childhood—the cruelty of Clara and Lily, the helplessness he felt as Richard endured their venom, and his struggles with guilt and anger. He didn't write to share it with his mother or sister, for he knew their rejection of him would only continue. They believed he sought to reclaim his place in the family or perhaps to claim an inheritance, a suspicion he found both painful and absurd. Instead, Ethan wrote for himself, using the act of writing to understand his emotions, confront his pain, and gain clarity on how to move forward.

Through this process, Ethan began to grow wiser. Reflecting on his past allowed him to see it in a new light—not to excuse it but to understand it. He realized that carrying anger toward Clara and Lily was like holding onto a burning coal; the fire did nothing to them but continued to scorch his hands. Slowly, he began to release the grip of resentment, not for their sake but for his freedom.

Forgive Them, Ethan!

Ethan visited Richard's grave one autumn afternoon as the golden leaves fell like confetti around him. He knelt beside the headstone, his fingers tracing the engraved letters of his father's name. The pain of loss swelled in his chest, but so did a sense of gratitude for his father's quiet strength, even in the face of adversity.

"Dad," Ethan whispered, his voice trembling with emotion. Tears streamed freely down his face, washing away years of pent-up sorrow. "I miss you so much. I think about you every day. I've been angry toward Mom and Lily, but I'm trying to let it go. I'm trying to forgive—not because they deserve it, but because I must move forward. I want to honor you by living free of this weight."

As the words left his lips, Ethan felt something shift within him. It was subtle, like the first rays of sunlight after a long storm. A sense of peace washed over him, soft and quiet but undeniable. He realized forgiveness wasn't about erasing the past or absolving those who wronged him. It was about releasing himself from the chains of anger and choosing to carry his father's memory with love rather than pain. For the first time in years, Ethan stood up from his father's grave feeling lighter, as though a significant burden had finally been lifted from his heart.

Several months later, a call came that Ethan never expected. Clara was on the line. Her voice, once sharp and commanding, sounded frail and hesitant. She wanted to meet. The request stirred a mix of emotions in Ethan—nervousness, hesitation, even a flicker of anger—but there was a quiet resolve beneath it all. He had spent so long preparing himself for this moment without knowing it. And so, he agreed.

When they finally sat across from one another, Ethan was struck by how much Clara had aged. Her once-proud demeanor had softened, and her face bore the marks of weariness and regret. There was no hostility in her eyes, only vulnerability. The conversation began cautiously as Ethan was unsure how to bridge the chasm of years and pain between them. But as they spoke, the walls started to crack, piece by piece.

They talked about Richard, their shared good memories, and the pain they had all endured in their ways. For the first time, Clara allowed herself to be raw and honest. Her hands trembled as she spoke, and her voice faltered, but her words carried the weight of sincerity.

"I'm sorry for everything, Ethan," she said, tears in her eyes. "I was so lost, so full of my bitterness, that I took it out on you and your father. I never wanted to hurt either of you, but I see now how much damage I caused. I don't expect forgiveness, but I wanted you to know I regret it all."

Ethan sat silently, the weight of her apology sinking in. The anger that had once been his constant companion felt distant now like a shadow retreating in the face of light. He took a deep breath, steadying his voice before responding.

"I've been angry for a long time, Mom," he said, his tone measured but compassionate. "I blamed you for so much. But I've learned that holding onto that anger doesn't help anyone—it just keeps me stuck in the past. I don't want to live like that anymore. I'm trying to forgive—not just you and Lily, but myself. I want to move forward for Dad and me."

Clara broke down at his words, her sobs shaking her frail frame. Ethan reached out, placing a hand on hers. It wasn't a moment of instant reconciliation, nor did it erase the years of pain, but it was a start. In that raw, vulnerable moment, mother and son took their first steps toward healing—not by forgetting the past, but by acknowledging it and leaving its weight behind. Ethan left that meeting feeling a quiet sense of closure. He didn't know the future of his relationship with Clara, but he knew he had done what he could to honor his father's memory and journey. He had chosen to forgive—not to absolve, but to free himself. In that freedom, he found the strength to continue building a life defined not by the pain of his past but by the hope of what lay ahead.

The Power of Forgiveness

ONCE shackled by the weight of his past, Ethan began to emerge from the suffocating shadows of resentment and self-doubt. Over time, he realized that true forgiveness wasn't about excusing his mother's actions or reopening the door to a relationship that had caused him so much pain. It was about releasing the heavy burden of the past, loosening its suffocating grip, and choosing to reclaim his peace.

Through this revelation, Ethan discovered that self-respect had to come first. It wasn't just about acknowledging his worth and learning to safeguard it. He began to set boundaries, not out of spite, but out of a desire to protect his emotional health. With this newfound clarity, he learned to prioritize his well-being, nurturing his spirit with kindness and filling his life with those who valued and cared for him genuinely.

The road to healing was neither quick nor easy. There were many difficult moments when vulnerability seemed like a weakness, and setbacks threatened to undo his progress. Yet with each challenge, Ethan grew stronger, more resilient, and more at peace with himself. In the quiet moments of solitude, he began to find solace. He rediscovered the beauty of small, simple joys—the sound of birds in the morning, the warmth of sunlight on his skin, the embrace of true friendship. These moments, once overlooked, now felt like lifelines to a life slowly being rebuilt.

Ethan's transformation wasn't a straight line. It wasn't an overnight change but a gradual unfolding, a deepening understanding of what it meant to heal. He learned to

Ethan's transformation wasn't a straight line. It wasn't an overnight change but a gradual unfolding, a deepening understanding of what it meant to heal. He learned to forgive, but not in the way he once imagined. He understood that forgiveness didn't require him to forget, nor did it demand reconciliation. It was simply releasing the past's hold on him, allowing him to move forward without being anchored by old wounds.

Emerging from the darkness, Ethan became a living testament to the strength of the human spirit. His healing journey illuminated a path for himself and others suffering in silence. He stood as a beacon of hope, proof that even in the most profound sorrow, the possibility of renewal exists.

The snow fell gently, a soft, unbroken white blanket reflecting the cold emptiness that had settled over the family. The town, a relic of a bygone era, was bound by tradition—its rigid social norms suffocated the individuality of its residents, stifling genuine emotions and connections.

At the heart of this frozen world was the family of Clara and Richard. Once vibrant and full of promise, their love had been slowly extinguished under societal pressures. Clara, a woman of quiet strength, had been forced to suppress her desires and ambitions, shaping herself into the woman society expected her to be. Richard, a man with deep, unspoken emotions, had struggled to express his love. His words, laden with fear and self-doubt, were often silenced by the looming judgment of those around him.

Their son, Ethan, grew up in the shadow of this unspoken pain. He longed for affection and understanding, craving a real connection with his parents. But their emotional distance left him feeling isolated, misunderstood, and alone. The town's suffocating atmosphere, where gossip was currency and

Texpectations were gospel, but they only deepened his alienation.

As Ethan matured, he began to rebel against the stifling norms of his upbringing, seeking solace in his unconventional path. His defiance, however, only widened the gap between him and his parents. To them, his choices seemed like a rejection of their values, a betrayal of the family's honor and tradition.

The cycle of misunderstanding and resentment continued, a tragic inheritance passed down through the generations. The family, once a source of love and support, had become a prison, its members trapped in a never-ending loop of emotional conflict. The town only perpetuated this cycle with its unwavering adherence to tradition, ensuring the tragedy would continue.

This family's story poignantly reminds us of the destructive power of societal expectations. It speaks to the heartbreaking consequences of living a life dictated by tradition rather than authentic emotion. Their tale is one of love lost, of dreams deferred, and of the human spirit's desperate struggle to break free from the suffocating chains of convention in search of its path to happiness.

Indeed, within the darkness of tradition, pain, and regret lies a quiet but undeniable force—the power of forgiveness and the desire to change. While the family's story has been marked by sorrow, resentment, and an unending cycle of emotional turmoil, the possibility for healing remains. Forgiveness, both of oneself and others offers a glimmer of hope that this painful cycle can be broken and a new path forged.

As Ethan began to work through his deep-seated anger, he understood that true forgiveness was not an act of excusing past wrongs but a release—a freedom from the heavy chains of resentment. When he realized this, he grasped the key to breaking the toxic loop that had bound his family for so long.

Forgiveness, while challenging, holds the power to heal not just the wounds inflicted by others but the self-inflicted pain that festers when bitterness takes root. In Ethan's case, forgiving his mother, Clara, and his sister, Lily, wasn't about forgetting their wrongs or condoning their behavior. It was about letting go of the anger that had consumed him and weighing the value of peace over the need for vengeance. It was the quiet decision to change the narrative —one written by a history of pain—and instead choose a future defined by growth, understanding, and self-respect.

The desire to change—the yearning for something different, something better—fuels the possibility of ending the harmful cycle. Ethan's emotional growth and gradual transformation were responses to forgiveness and conscious choices to evolve. This desire for change transformed him, allowing him to see his past for what it truly was: a chapter that, while painful, no longer had to dictate the rest of his life.

And so, the bad cycle—one rooted in inherited trauma, misunderstanding, and emotional neglect—began to loosen its grip. By choosing forgiveness, Ethan found the courage to reclaim his life. He understood that breaking free from this cycle would not come from blaming others but from healing himself and embracing the love he had long sought, not from others but within.

Thus, The family's story shifts from despair to possibility. Through forgiveness, Ethan closed the chapter of unresolved pain and opened a new one filled with hope. The realization that change was possible—within him, the family, and the town itself —was the first step in breaking the chains of the past and moving forward into a future where the cycle of hurt and resentment could finally be archived. The power of forgiveness became the bridge to healing, offering not just closure but the promise of a better tomorrow, free from the shadows of the past.

Takeaways

THE story of Ethan and his family offers several profound takeaways, each offering insights into human emotions, the power of healing, and the importance of personal growth:

1. The Power of Forgiveness: One of the central messages is that forgiveness is not about excusing harmful behavior but about freeing oneself from the burden of anger and resentment. Forgiveness allows healing for the individual and, potentially, relationships. It's about letting go of the past to reclaim peace and happiness.

2. Self-Respect and Boundaries: Ethan's journey demonstrates the importance of recognizing one's worth and setting boundaries. The story shows that personal growth and healing often come from learning to prioritize one's well-being, even in the face of painful relationships.

3. The Impact of Societal Expectations: The story critiques the destructive power of rigid societal norms and their pressure on individuals, especially within families. It underscores how these external forces can stifle authentic emotion, personal growth, and connection. The family's suffering is a cautionary tale about the dangers of living up to expectations at the expense of personal truth.

4. Generational Trauma and the Possibility of Breaking the Cycle: The cycle of pain that stretches across generations in Ethan's family is a stark reminder of how trauma can be passed down. However, it also offers hope that this cycle can be broken. Change and healing start with the willingness to reflect, acknowledge the past, and make conscious choices to heal and evolve.

5. The Importance of Emotional Vulnerability: Both Richard's journal entries and Ethan's growth highlight the strength found in vulnerability. Embracing vulnerability through self-reflection, therapy, or confronting past wounds is a critical step toward understanding oneself and others and achieving emotional freedom.

6. Personal Growth is a Journey: Healing and personal transformation are not immediate; they are gradual processes. Ethan's story teaches that growth often comes with setbacks, vulnerability, and patience. It's a continual journey; taking it one step at a time is okay.

7. Releasing the Past to Move Forward: The story conveys that while the past shapes us, it does not have to define us. Letting go of the weight of old wounds and unresolved issues is necessary to build a future free from the chains of previous trauma.

8. The Desire for Connection: At its core, this is a story about the human need for genuine connection—whether with family, friends, or oneself. Ethan's search for love and understanding shows how deeply we long for authentic relationships and how toxic relationships can cloud that need. His journey is ultimately about creating healthier connections, starting with himself.

These takeaways point toward the profound potential of healing, growth, and the ability to shape one's future, no matter how painful the past may be. They offer hope for those grappling with family dynamics, emotional wounds, and the quest for personal peace.

Reflection Questions

1. What role did societal expectations play in Clara's decisions throughout the story?
   - Societal expectations pressured Clara to marry and fulfill her role as a wife and mother, contributing to her internal conflicts and dissatisfaction.
2. How did Richard's character influence the dynamics within the family?
   - Richard's calm demeanor and unconditional love starkly contrast Clara's resentment, ultimately leading to a toxic environment for Ethan.
3. In what ways did Ethan's journey toward forgiveness reflect his personal growth?
   - Ethan's journey highlighted his ability to confront his pain, understand his family's complexities, and ultimately choose forgiveness to reclaim his happiness.
4. What lessons can be drawn about the importance of communication in family relationships?
   - Open communication is essential for understanding and healing. The lack of it in Clara and Richard's relationship contributed to the family's dysfunction.
5. How can forgiveness impact mental health and overall well-being?
   - Forgiveness can alleviate anger and resentment, improving mental health, healthier relationships, and peace.

Practicing forgiveness

FOR someone dealing with similar issues as Ethan—where family dynamics, past trauma, or unresolved anger are affecting their well-being—practicing forgiveness can be an essential step in their healing journey. Here are several practices of forgiveness that could help:

1.Acknowledge and Accept the Hurt
Before forgiveness can occur, it's important to acknowledge the hurt and pain caused by the actions of others. Denying or suppressing feelings only prolongs the suffering. This involves being honest with oneself about the depth of the emotional wound and accepting that it has impacted one's life in meaningfully.

2. Separate the Person from the Behavior
Forgiveness doesn't mean excusing harmful behavior but rather separating the person from their actions. This allows individuals to understand that while someone may have hurt them, it doesn't define who they are. Recognizing this can create space for empathy and help release the anger tied to specific actions.

3. Recognize the Power of Letting Go
One key component of forgiveness is the understanding that holding onto anger or resentment only prolongs the suffering and prevents personal growth. Letting go of these feelings doesn't mean condoning the wrong; it simply means releasing their toxic grip on one's life.

4. Write it Down: Letters or Journaling

Writing a letter (even if you never send it) can be incredibly therapeutic to express anger, hurt, and feelings of abandonment. Journaling can also help one process emotions in a safe, private space. Writing allows individuals to voice their pain without fear of judgment or misunderstanding.

If writing a letter to the person involved feels too overwhelming, tell yourself how the situation made you feel, what your needs are, and what you wish could have happened differently.

5. Practice Self-Forgiveness

Sometimes, the most challenging part of forgiveness is forgiving oneself. Individuals might feel guilt or shame for not protecting themselves or their perceived failings. Learning to forgive oneself is a crucial part of healing. Recognizing that everyone makes mistakes and that these mistakes do not define your worth is essential for moving forward.

6. Empathy and Perspective-Taking

Try to view the situation from the other person's perspective. This doesn't mean agreeing with their actions but understanding their potential motivations or struggles. Perhaps the person who hurt you was acting out of their pain or fear. Developing empathy doesn't excuse the behavior but helps create understanding and soften the heart.

7. Therapy and Professional Support

Seeking therapy, either individually or as part of family counseling, can provide a safe environment to work through deep-seated issues. A trained therapist can guide individuals through difficult emotions, offer coping strategies, and help facilitate the process of forgiveness.

Group therapy or support groups where others share similar experiences can also be a helpful resource for building a sense of community and understanding.

8. Set Boundaries with Compassion

Forgiveness doesn't require reconciliation or maintaining a close relationship with the person who caused the pain. It's important to set healthy boundaries to protect oneself from further harm. Boundaries can be set with compassion—acknowledging that you are choosing to forgive and protecting your emotional well-being.

9. Mindfulness and Meditation

Mindfulness and meditation can be powerful tools for managing negative emotions and increasing self-awareness. These practices help individuals stay grounded in the present moment, allowing them to observe their thoughts and feelings without judgment or attachment. Over time, mindfulness can help reduce the emotional charge of past traumas.

10. Release Expectations

Often, we hold on to anger because we expect someone to apologize or change their behavior. However, expecting another person to take responsibility can sometimes delay our healing. By releasing the expectation of how the other person should respond, individuals can focus more on their healing process rather than waiting for validation.

11. Give Time

Forgiveness is rarely instantaneous. Healing from deep emotional wounds takes time and patience. One must allow time to process the pain rather than rush toward forgiveness. Recognizing that this is a gradual journey can prevent feelings of frustration or self-blame when progress feels slow.

12. Gratitude Practice

Engaging in a gratitude practice can shift one's mindset from focusing on what was lost or wrong to appreciating the positive aspects of life. Being grateful for small victories, supportive relationships, or personal growth can shift the energy around forgiveness and promote healing.

13. Focus on Your Growth

Use the process of forgiveness as an opportunity for personal growth. Focus on becoming the person you want to be, independent of the past. Invest in building your self-worth, self-care, and healthy relationships. The more one cultivates self-love and strength, the easier it becomes to release negative emotions tied to others.

These practices can help create a path toward healing, not only through forgiving others but also by empowering oneself. It's important to note that forgiveness is not about forgetting or excusing bad behavior; it's about finding peace and freeing oneself from the chains of unresolved anger. It is ultimately an act of self-compassion.

Poignant quotes

On Forgiveness:
"To forgive is to set a prisoner free and discover that the prisoner was you." — Lewis Smedes
"Forgiveness is not about forgetting; it's about letting go." — Unknown
"The weak can never forgive. Forgiveness is the attribute of the strong." — Mahatma Gandhi

On Love and Relationships:
"Love is not a feeling; it is a commitment. It's not about what you feel, it's about what you do." — Unknown
"The greatest happiness of life is the conviction that we are loved, loved for ourselves, or rather, loved despite ourselves." — Victor Hugo
"Love is patient, love is kind. It does not envy, it does not boast, it is not proud. It does not dishonor others, it is not self-seeking, it is not easily angered, it keeps no record of wrongs." — 1 Corinthians 13:4-5

On Human Nature and the Power of the Human Spirit:
"The human spirit is stronger than any adversity." — William James
"In the depth of winter, I finally learned that within me there lay an invincible summer." — Albert Camus
"The only way to deal with heartache is to keep busy. Work, work, work. Keep working and let time pass." — Maya Angelou

Disclaimer Notice

The information in this document is for educational and entertainment purposes only. All efforts have been made to show accurate, up-to-date, reliable, and complete information. No warranties of any kind are declared or implied. I just wanted to let you know that the author is not engaged in rendering legal, financial, medical, or professional advice. The content within this book has been derived from various sources. Please look at a licensed professional before you try any techniques outlined in this book. This book was crafted using AI technology to enhance clarity, research, and content organization.

Notes

Liudmila Pirojenko

COULD YOU TAKE A MOMENT TO SHARE YOUR THOUGHTS IN A REVIEW?

I would be incredibly grateful
It truly helps

Author Bio

 **LIUDMILA PIROJENKO**, MA in Languages, is a Teacher and Translator. Due to the specifics of her profession, she often has to deal with the problems presented in this book

Contact: LinkedIn account https://www.linkedin.com/in/liud mila-pir/

Travel Italy Newsletter: https://exegi.substack.com/
Mystery in Life Newsletter https://mystery-life.beehiiv.com

For Reviews, please visit
Amazon Author's Page
https://www.amazon.com/stores/Liudmila-Pirojenko/author/B0DK91G1JW

www.ingramcontent.com/pod-product-compliance
Lightning Source LLC
Chambersburg PA
CBHW051718250726

48653CB00008B/3090